Times Gone By

With classic photographs from
The Francis Frith Collection

Times Gone By

With classic photographs from The Francis Frith Collection

SELECT
EDITIONS

Selectabook
Devizes

First published in the United Kingdom in 2005 by
Black Horse Books
for Selectabook Limited, Devizes

ISBN 1-84546-334-X

British Library Cataloguing in Publication Data

Times Gone By – With classic photographs from The Francis Frith Collection

Black Horse Books
Frith's Barn, Teffont,
Salisbury, Wiltshire SP3 5QP
Tel: +44 (0) 1722 716 376
Email: info@francisfrith.co.uk
www.francisfrith.co.uk

Printed and bound in China

Front Cover: East Molesey, 'Coming Over the Rollers' 1896 38346t
Frontispiece: Oxford, Cornmarket Street 1922 71996

The colour-tinting in this book is for illustrative purposes only, and is not intended to be historically accurate

Contents

Earning a Living

PENNY HILL PARK 1906
Bagshot, Surrey 57177

Gardeners tend the remarkable holly hedge of Penny Hill Park, which grows in places up to 40 feet high. Penny Hill Park was built in 1873, and is now a hotel. It has a beautifully landscaped garden.

THE KITCHEN GARDEN 1911
Pell Wall Hall, Shropshire 63372

Forcing plants and flowers in the kitchen garden reached its zenith in the 19th century, offering hosts considerable scope for impressing their guests. As well as providing vegetables and fruit all year round, it grew exotic blooms to decorate the rooms of the house – often these were chosen to complement the colours of the ladies' gowns. This ceaseless quest for the exotic and unlikely generated a tremendous amount of work for the gardeners.

ONION SELLERS 1907
Plymouth, Devon 59208

This charming study of two young onion sellers was taken by the Frith photographer during the long and prosperous 'Edwardian afternoon'. Merchant ships brought goods from all over the world into Plymouth's harbours.

THE KNIFE GRINDER 1906
Hartfield, Hertfordshire 56692

Here we see a knife grinder at work in this atmospheric picture of a deserted Hartfield. It is a delightful village on the northern edge of Ashdown Forest above the river Medway. Today Hartfield is best known for its association with Winnie-the-Pooh, whose creator, A A Milne, lived for many years at nearby Cotchford Farm.

The streets of London used to be thronged with beggars, confidence tricksters and street traders. Here we see a chair mender squatting in the passage outside the kitchen of a London house. There were once 2,500 cabinet making shops in London, many employing children. When powered sawmills and mechanical production methods brought ready-made furniture onto the market, many thousands of craftsmen lost their jobs. This old man re-canes a child's chair, while the housekeeper maintains a wary eye.

CHAIR MENDER 1877
London L130112

8

CLAYPITS POTTERY 1937
Ewenny, Mid Glamorgan 87908

Arthur Trevorrow is throwing a jug on the wheel; beside him are various examples of his work, beautifully hand-decorated with slip in waves, whorls and dots. On the right, William Jenkins, the proprietor of Claypits Pottery, holds a jug ready for his nephew Tom Jenkins (centre) to decorate – Tom was to take over the business in 1939. Such a scene had been commonplace in Ewenny for over 300 years. At one stage there were a dozen small family potteries here, owing to deposits of earthenware clay nearby.

LACE WORKER 1901
Beer, South Devon 47861

A lace maker works at a floral sprig of Honiton lace outside her cottage door at Beer in South Devon. If the picture had been taken a few years earlier, her customer might have been Queen Victoria herself. The queen helped revive the Devon lace industry by making lace fashionable again; among her commissions was the flounce for her wedding dress, which was made by a hundred of the finest lace makers in Devon.

THE POSTMEN 1936
Clovelly, Devon 87551

Outside the Higher Clovelly post office, postman Roy Fisher accepts the sacks of local post from the Bideford van. Beside him stands the post donkey, who was vital to efficient and regular deliveries in this isolated village in North Devon. Clovelly clings to a cliff, and its street is a steep, cobbled flight of steps. Villagers still use donkeys and sleds to carry goods to and from their cottages and the tiny harbour far below.

QUEEN VICTORIA STREET 1897
London L130055

City life seems as hectic in the 1890s as it does today. Richard Jefferies describes the frenetic scene in his 1883 book 'The Story of My Heart': 'Streams of human life flow into this agitated pool of blue carts and yellow omnibuses, varnished carriages and brown vans … men and women fill the interstices between the carriages and blacken the surface, till the vans almost float on human beings … This is the vortex and whirlpool, the centre of human life today on the earth. Here it seethes and whirls, not for an hour only, but for all present time, hour by hour, day by day, year by year'.

THE BANK OF ENGLAND 1890
London L130179

The 1881 census revealed a steady rise in the size of the professional, commercial and managerial classes: in 1890 the city's fortunes were founded not on industrial might but on the realm of international finance. London was the banking capital of the world, and this is reflected by the bustling City scene shown here, with the imposing Bank of England in the background.

HOKEY-POKEY STALL 1884
Greenwich, London L130110

Small children cluster round the hokey-pokey stall, gleefully licking at the cheap ice cream. They look like ragged street urchins in their rumpled clothes and battered boots, and were probably bought their penny treats in return for posing for the photographer. The stallholder, standing to the right in his apron and straw hat, is no more than a youth, and is probably one of many hired hands working for a much larger concern.

For us today, with water spurting from taps in sinks, basins and baths, it is hard to imagine the time and labour that used to be involved in collecting and fetching water. Buckets slung on yokes were used in prehistoric times, and were still being used by the Victorians. Going to the stream or well was a daily task, and carrying the buckets was hard work, especially after a day spent working in the fields. The water seller was a regular caller at many dry, heathland villages, where water was at a premium. Here we see him filling a cottager's bucket with water from his barrel.

THE WATER SELLER 1888
Haslemere, Surrey H35501

AN OLD COCKLE WOMAN 1906
Exmouth, Devon 53961

This old woman is 'scratting' (scratching) the sands for the dark-coloured Devon cockles. She is watching for the tell-tale pair of small holes which betray the cockle's presence an inch or so below the surface. Her cuffs are cut away to prevent them from drawing cold seawater up her arms, her skirt is tucked up, and her scarf is tied tight around her hat. With her stockings cut away at the ankles, she paddles barefoot in the freezing water, bent double for hours on end. Back in the village, she will sell her cockles to the fishmonger, keeping a few back for her dinner.

THE VILLAGE SMITHY c1920
Exford, Somerset E50501

By the 1920s, many smiths had ceased to tend horses, but tended cars instead – they had made the transition from farrier to motor mechanic. But the Exford smith is still carrying on his traditional business, although his forge has seen better days – the thatch has worn wafer thin and will soon be letting in water. The rickety door is smothered with auctioneers' flyers for farm sales; the village forge had always been a meeting place for farmers where they could gossip and discuss the news of the day.

FISHWIVES 1890
Tenby, Dyfed 28091

These fishwives have been shrimping with nets on the sands and filling the baskets they carry on their backs. They have been paddling in the shallows on South Beach, facing the broad seaward sweep that takes in Caldy Island and the Gower Peninsula. The old walled town of Tenby was a highly popular watering-place in the far south-west of Wales, and the women will find plenty of customers when they hawk their catch on the beach and quayside. They are wearing traditional Welsh shawls draped around their shoulders and long heavy skirts.

NOMADS 1885
London L130212

The nameless, faceless gypsies came and went, selling their wares wherever they travelled. There would be rich pickings in London. The working classes were very superstitious and, although wary of the gypsies, their curiosity would get the better of them and they would pay to buy the wares or have their palms read.

A SELF-BINDER AT WORK 1920
Lustleigh, Devon 69626

We tend to think that period photographs of farming scenes portray a countryside that was an unchanging and eternal rural idyll. Yet from the late Victorian period, the fields were an arena in which fundamental changes were taking place. Brand new inventions, tools and machinery were displacing the manual labourer, and an era was nearing its end. This beautiful view shows a reaping scene with a self-binder. This device cut the oats, drew them into sheaves and tied them. Self-binders are still used today for binding wheat sheaves for thatchers – modern combines crush the stems, destroying their waterproof qualities and durability.

Country Life

A SHEEP SALE ON THE GREEN
c1910
Malham, Yorkshire M139023

At the time when this photograph was taken, the village green at Malham was the scene of regular sheep sales attended by farmers from the surrounding fells. The crammed pens full of white-nosed Swaledale sheep are critically inspected by the bowler-hatted farmers, who would undoubtedly haggle over the price they expected to get or pay.

IN THE HOP FIELD 1904
Goudhurst, Kent 52571D

In many villages in Kent are the great gardens and oast-houses devoted to the growing and processing of the hop, which gives beer its taste. At hop harvest, armies of the London poor travelled out to enjoy a few weeks of healthy open-air labour. In this picture, the pickers pose in the dappled shade.

A FLOWER FARM c1891

The Scilly Isles S73303

In about 1870, William Trevillick packed a few home-grown Scilly White narcissi in his Aunt Ellen's hatbox and sent them over the Channel to Covent Garden. They made 7/6. Delighted and surprised – for there was little public demand for cut flowers at the time – he sent some more. From this unlikely beginning grew the world-famous flower industry of the Scillies. Here we see the half-opened blooms being picked in spring – this was traditionally men's work; women and children did the bunching, tying and packing.

This is a fine old Sussex downland post mill with a domesticated structure enclosing the trestle. Powered by two common cloth sails and two spring-controlled sails, the mill was turned into the wind by means of a tailpole. It was built in around 1710 and worked to 1894, and again until 1914. The photograph shows the mill when the site was used as a tea garden. The mill is now restored to working order, with an original-style roundhouse enclosing the trestle, and is open to visitors.

THE OLD MILL 1919
High Salvington, Sussex

68994

THE VILLAGE CORNER c1960
Bishop Burton, Yorkshire B427002

This unforgettable village cupped in a hollow with a large wayside pond is the home of All Saints' Church. In the chancel is a chalice brass to Vicar Johnson, 1460, one of the earliest examples of this kind of brass work. There is also a bust of John Wesley carved from an elm that grew on the green where he preached.

THE MILL 1910
Cropthorne, Worcestershire 62353

Situated on the Avon, Cropthorne Mill has often attracted the attentions of artists and photographers. The woman and child are crossing the river by way of a chain ferry, pulling themselves across on a fixed cable – almost the oldest form of regular river crossing in England.

THE VILLAGE 1921
Downham, Lancashire 71189

In this carefully composed picture we see the lower part of the village. The two men, one holding the horse and one with his dog, are everything a photographer could want in a village scene. The two ladies sitting on the grass add charm to the picture, which is typical of Downham; it is a well managed, working village that has not forgotten its history. The 15th century church has some very fierce-looking gargoyles.

HIGH STREET 1900
Skipton, Yorkshire 45756

Here we see a busy market day. In the background is the parish church, which contains some elaborate monuments to the Clifford family, the Earls of Cumberland. During the siege of the castle, the church was badly damaged, but it was restored by Lady Anne Clifford before she died in 1675.

FISHING 1926
Grassington, Yorkshire 79062

Grassington was at one time a centre for lead mining, but by 1900 it was once again reliant upon agriculture, athough there was still some quarrying in the locality. The railway finally came to the village in 1902 with the opening of a line to Skipton. Here we see a quiet moment on the banks of the Wharfe.

THE BARLEY MOW INN 1890
Clifton Hampden, Oxfordshire
27010

Standing on the east bank of the Thames, below the bridge, this medieval inn is noted for its cruck construction – note the large curved timbers in the gable wall – and for the fact that Jerome K Jerome commends the inn in 'Three Men in a Boat'. The timbers are now painted black rather that being (correctly) limewashed as in this view. A house now stands behind.

The old gnarled trees add character to this idyllic setting. Selworthy Green is now owned by the National Trust. The thatched cottages were erected in 1828 by Sir Thomas Dyke Acland for his retired estate workers. Many of the cottages have survived, retaining their original charm.

THE GREEN 1883
Selworthy, Somerset

15836

THE VILLAGE 1904
Streatley, Berkshire 52933

Streatley lies at the junction of several major routes as they converge on the Goring Gap. The Bull at Streatley public house is on the left. Here the characters in Jerome K Jerome's 'Three Men in a Boat' lunched, accompanied by their dog. The lunch was, apparently, 'much to Montmorency's satisfaction'. On the extreme right, Wells's grocer shop has a fine gilded glass signboard.

33

THE FERRY INN 1888
Bodinnick, Cornwall 21236

Bodinnick is a tiny village built on a steep hill on one side of Pont Creek, an estuary of the Fowey River. From here the ferryboats would take the passengers across the fast-flowing river to Fowey. Daphne du Maurier, the famous authoress, stayed here when still a young girl, and often lunched with her parents at this quaint inn. The du Maurier family still own a house alongside the inn at the water's edge. The cottages above the Ferry Inn are a joyous sight in summer, their gardens packed tight with bright flowers.

HIGH STREET 1890
Newhaven, Sussex 27760

Newhaven developed as the 'new town' after the River Ouse shifted its mouth in 1579. The mouth was stabilised in 1733, and there were great plans for the port. By the 1880s, it was the sixth most important port in the country. The promise has never been truly fulfilled. This cheerful scene shows the old town, little of which still stands, with awnings and pot plants and an intriguing advertisement for Tit-Bits.

Town Life

THE MARKET 1901
Hitchin, Hertfordshire 46633

The bustling twice-weekly market was clearly a popular event at the turn of the century. The cupola of the 1851 Corn Exchange rises above the collection of stalls and the surrounding Georgian facades. The flint-faced post office is on the right. Note the lone policeman keeping a watchful eye on events in the right foreground.

**HOME & COLONIAL
STORES 1914**
Station Road, Harrow-on-the-Hill, Middlesex 66820

Here we see the beginnings of a familiar retail pattern: multinationals are taking over the high street. On the left is Home & Colonial, which by this date had several hundred branches. Their pricing policy was aggressive: signs in the window proclaim '2d in the shilling returned'. Two doors along is Boots, 'the largest chemist in the world', and just beyond that Sainsbury's, with its distinctive shop interiors, spacious, practical and hygienic, worlds away from the small, cramped corner shop of old.

MARKET PLACE 1922
Banbury, Oxfordshire
72090

*R*obins Brothers, not content with filling their windows to bursting, have extended out on to the pavement and into the road. This was an era when labour-saving machines of all kinds were being invented for the home and garden. Next door, the silent film version of 'The Count of Monte Cristo' is showing.

THE MARKET HALL 1896
Halifax, Yorkshire 38782

Halifax's red brick market was constructed in the 1890s. Inside there was space for 43 shops and over 100 stalls. In addition, a fish market offered sixteen choice counters. Shoppers could purchase all their weekly goods here, from hardware to the freshest vegetables. The magnificent cast-iron pillars held up the glass roof, giving welcome natural light to the interior of the busy Borough Market.

CORNMARKET STREET 1922
Oxford, Oxfordshire 71996

The most striking building amid the shops is the rough-hewn late Anglo-Saxon tower of St Michael's Church, with its two tiers of paired belfry windows. To the right, the tall gabled building of 1915 is still occupied by WH Smith, but there have been some losses on the left side of the street, which is now partly pedestrianised.

LONG ROW EAST 1902
Nottingham, Nottinghamshire 48326

This bustling scene offers a microcosm of life a century ago. Though it seems we are looking back into an era long past, already the trams are electric-powered. However, the cabs and carts are still relying on horse-power. Note the complexity of building styles along the street line – the Victorians had no concern for harmony or for what was appropriate.

KING WILLIAM STREET 1880
London L130102

Here we are at the junction of Cannon Street and the approach to the new London Bridge; the street was opened by King William IV in 1831, and named after him. In 1844 a statue of William IV was erected to the right of where this view ends. On the left is the City Luncheon Bar, and passing in the foreground carriers' carts, two owned by Henry Draper and another by the railway.

Sports and Leisure

THE EIGHTS 1922
Oxford, Oxfordshire 72063

The Thames, or Isis, plays an important role in Oxford university life. Here, we are on the tow path along the west bank, looking north towards Christchurch Meadow; it is the end of May, and the annual Eights Week, when the college boats race each other, is in full swing. Spectators in up-to-the-minute fashions look on from the shore and from punts.

DARTMOUTH REGATTA 1889
Dartmouth, Devon 21648

Dartmouth is still very much a sailing town, and the Royal Regatta, which is held annually in August, still attracts huge crowds. Of course, nowadays the craft are quite different to the sailing vessels in the photograph. The social life within the yacht clubs and the river attracts many naval officers to live out their retirement here.

THE COLLEGE PLAYING FIELDS 1907
Cheltenham, Gloucestershire 59038

A sizeable crowd are fully engrossed in the action of a cricket match on the playing fields of the school, against the backdrop of the buildings, all of which are contained on an 85-acre site. The school was founded in 1841. The crowded stand, erected in front of the yellow brick gymnasium with its two towers, indicates that this is probably a match between county teams held during the annual Cheltenham Cricket Festival, rather than one between Cheltenham College sides.

$\mathcal{M}$odern golfers benefit from the latest technology: an aerodynamic ball, and well-balanced clubs made from a precise blend of metals. How well might today's professionals perform with a 'featherie', the ball used until 1850? Made from boiled feathers, it was about as aerodynamic as a haggis. Golf was hardly played outside Scotland until the 1860s, when the first English club, the North Devon at Westward Ho!, was formed. At the Mullion course, pictured here, golfers could hear the thundering of the waves on the rocks and enjoy the sea breezes. Golfing dress – Norfolk jacket and breeches – was refreshingly informal in a society which prided itself on its propriety.

THE GOLF LINKS 1911
Mullion, Cornwall 64023

THE TENNIS COURTS 1886
Buxton, Derbyshire 18659

These women players are at a considerable disadvantage with their long, billowing dresses and broad-brimmed headgear. The Victorian tennis authorities had suggested that the ball should be allowed to bounce twice to give the ladies time to get about the court, but the idea was rejected. However, ladies were allowed to serve underarm – if they had made any attempt at over-arm serving they would have knocked off their hats. It was considered very bad form to volley or smash, and lobbing was unheard-of.

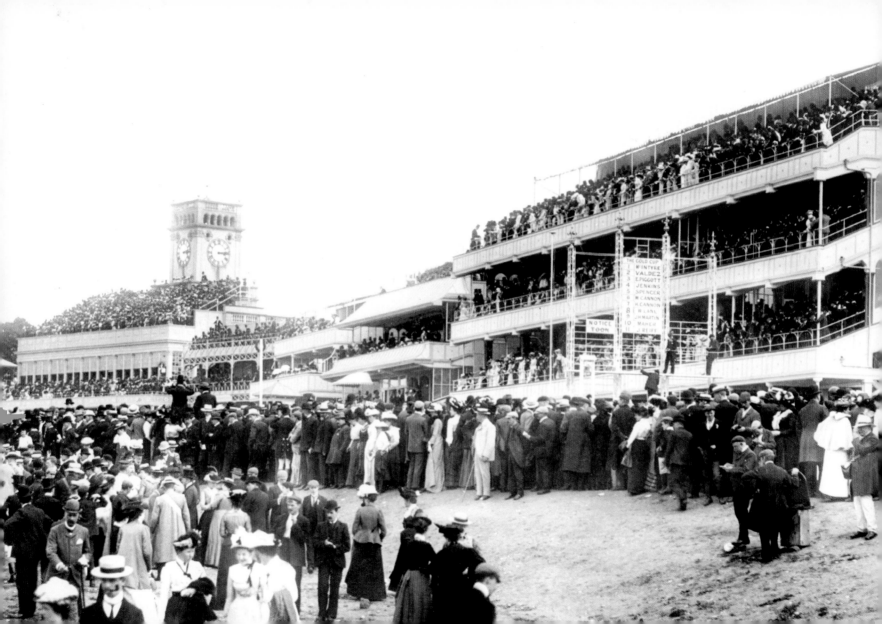

THE GRANDSTAND 1902
Ascot Racecourse, Berkshire 48276

After the death of his mother Queen Victoria, Edward VII did much to promote Ascot as a significant social event. This photograph of the racecourse was taken a year after Edward became King. Queen Anne established this famous racecourse in 1711, though the meetings only became popular when the Duke of Cumberland revived them later in the 18th century.

COMING OVER THE ROLLERS 1896
The River Thames, East Molesey, Surrey 38346

River outings on the Thames were popular in Victorian times. Jerome K Jerome describes a classic journey in his 'Thee Men in a Boat'. He tells of the bedlam at Molesey, where 'you could not see any water at all, but only a brilliant tangle of bright blazers, and gay caps, and saucy hats, and many-coloured parasols, … and streaming ribbons, and dainty whites'. This photograph depicts pure pandemonium, with punts and skiffs forcing their passage in every direction.

THE SWAN HOTEL 1899
Streatley, Berkshire 42994

Here we are granted a vision of pure peace. A boatman is resting his oars while hotel guests sit contemplating the slow-moving river. This rambling old inn is now the Swan Diplomat Hotel; the main building is much extended to the right, the left and the front. The thatched room is now tiled, and the outbuilding to the left converted to hotel rooms. To the right is now moored one of the Oxford college barges.

THE MILL AND THE RIVER c1934
The Broads, Norfolk

T213064

This quiet scene shows a drainage tower mill starting to fall into disrepair: two blades of the fantail are missing. The patent sails appear to be empty of shutters. By this time, land drainage had mainly been entrusted to engine and electrically-driven pumps, rendering windmill pumps obsolete, and only kept as a landscape feature.

THE STONE PIER 1900
Aberdour, Fife 45912

A packed steamer is kept firmly alongside the pier as the Master on the bridge plots her progress carefully. She is either about to put warps ashore or has just taken them aboard. The length of the boat is fairly substantial compared to the head of the jetty, so she requires delicate and careful manoeuvring if she is to be handled safely.

THE FERRY BOAT 1896
Bowness, Cumbria 38800

The Bowness ferry carries a coach and four across Lake Windermere. The horses are steadied from the front by the ferryman, and the driver holds the reins in case the animals bolt: it is a chain ferry, drawn through the water by a steam-driven boat alongside, so a sudden hiss might startle the team. The well-to-do passengers silently contemplate the sublime fells made famous by the poet Wordsworth, enjoying the broad, breezy prospects.

BOLTON ABBEY 1886
Yorkshire 18510

A young woman watches her husband painting a watercolour. In the background are the romantic ruins of the Augustinian priory, and to the right are the tumbling waters of the River Wharfe. Turner and Landseer are just two of the many painters who have been drawn to the sublime scenery around the abbey. Bolton Abbey is rich in prospects for the artistic eye: there are the stepping stones across the river, the deep green hanging woods, the lively bubbling waters, and the ancient stones of the abbey itself.

THE WISHING WELL 1923
Upwey, Dorset 73960

Upwey stands on the high road between Weymouth and Dorchester and features in Thomas Hardy's novel 'The Trumpet Major'. The famous wishing well was a favourite day out for early visitors to Weymouth, who would taste the water and think of their heart's desire. A shack nearby provided simple refreshments, and the tourists would sit on the surrounding benches.

MARKET PLACE 1912
Ambleside, Cumbria 64302

Here we see a busy scene at the height of the tourist season. Queues are forming, and visitors are clambering aboard horse-drawn coaches that will carry them out into a picturesque world of lakes and mountains. Many of the coach tours to Keswick and Windermere are advertised on hoardings along the street.

THE STEPPING STONES 1888
Ambleside, Cumbria 20484

Ambleside is situated at the centre of the Lake District; this is now a haven for walkers, and a very busy place in the summer months. Here a lady negotiates the stepping stones with trepidation. She probably wonders how she is going to keep her long skirts dry. The stones still lie on the riverbed between Rydal and Ambleside.

THE CRYSTAL PALACE c1890
London C207020

After the Great Exhibition of 1851, the Crystal Palace was moved to Sydenham in south-east London, where it was filled with lavish displays. The grounds around it were transformed into fantastic gardens with temples, pleasure walks, lakes with islands and fountains, a maze, a grotto, groves and lawns. It became a paradise of leisure for Londoners, who flocked to enjoy the special displays and exhibitions, including firework displays by Messrs Brock that lit up the sky with 5,000 rockets, and an appearance by Blondin, who walked the high wire and cooked an omelette seventy feet up in the air.

HYDE PARK c1890
London L130330

Hyde Park is the largest green area in central London. It was originally one of Henry VIII's deer parks, and was primarily used for hunting. The park was opened to the public in the 17th century. Here, on Rotten Row, the fashionable and the elegant mingle to gossip and show off.

BACTRIAN CAMEL 1913
Regent's Park Zoo, London
65251

Founded by the Zoological Society of London in grounds laid out by the architect Decimus Burton, the Regent's Park Zoo opened its doors to the public in 1828. Early visitors were confronted for the first time with exotic bears, kangaroos, zebras, llamas and an ostrich. It seems odd to us today that the public were encouraged to feed them: there was a stall selling cakes, fruits and nuts. Thirty thousand Londoners visited in the first six months. In 1840, a kangaroo escaped, causing havoc as it hopped energetically amongst the panicking visitors.

PELICANS 1913
Regent's Park Zoo, London
65252

VALLEY GARDENS 1907
Harrogate, Yorkshire 58645

Harrogate is one of the oldest of England's spa towns: its mineral springs were discovered in the 16th century. During the 19th and early 20th century, Harrogate was highly fashionable and very popular. Valley Gardens was a favourite place for a mild constitutional after taking the waters. Here a small crowd enjoys an afternoon concert given by a Pierrot troupe; this type of entertainment owed its popularity to the runaway success of the London production of the mime play 'L'Enfant Prodigue' in 1891, in which the character of Pierrot featured. The act would include songs, jokes, mime and monologues.

CRESCENT GARDENS 1907
Harrogate, Yorkshire 58648

For decades, music was a feature of everyday life during the Harrogate season. Late morning concerts were held both at the Crescent and the Winter Gardens. In 1896 a Municipal Orchestra was formed under the leadership of J Sydney Jones; it survived until it was disbanded as an economy measure in 1930.

INVALID'S WALK 1900
Bournemouth, Dorset 45225

A contemporary guide book extolled Bournemouth's climate: 'it is perhaps most beneficial to invalids during the fall of the year and the early spring, when it will compare favourably with many of the Mediterranean resorts. Here the sick and infirm could sit in the sun-dappled shadows of the town's beautiful gardens. They could promenade along the paths, taking gentle, healing exercise.

THE CONVALESCENT HOME 1887
Lowestoft, Suffolk 19856

Lowestoft's convalescent home was a gift to the town in 1877 from William Birbeck, who was himself ill – he died in 1897. Here some of the staff and patients are having a game of croquet on the front lawn while others look on, perhaps enjoying the benefits of a sunny day.

A MARCHING BAND 1917
Frensham, Surrey F47330

This haunting and unusual picture shows a marching band at Frensham during the First World War. How many of these men came back wounded to be cared for at Frensham Military Hospital, based at a large mansion, Frensham Heights? How many were to return alive by the end of the following year? Frensham is known for its ponds and its common – now Frensham Country Park.

By the Seaside

THE CENTRAL PIER 1890
Blackpool, Lancashire 22881

The pier opened in 1868 as the South Pier, then changed its name to Blackpool Central when the Victoria (now South) Pier opened. Over the years it became known as the 'People's Pier', specialising in a vast range of amusement activities. A more genteel pier would not have been so covered in advertisements!

THE PIER 1910
Eastbourne, Sussex 62958

Designed by Eugenius Birch, the doyen of pier architects, the pier opened in 1870. Its first theatre seated 400, and cost a mere £250 – it eventually became a cattle-shed at Lewes! The saloons visible here halfway along the decking were added in 1901, the same year that work on the new pavilion was completed.

ROUGH SEAS, FROM THE PIER 1890
Bognor Regis, Sussex 25182B

Bognor was described thus in a Victorian tourist 1895 guidebook: 'This town is Worthing's twin sister – a quiet, mild, healthy watering-place, situate on a level in the face of the ever-restless Channel. The Local Board have expended £14,000 on a sea-wall and fine esplanade, and the pier, 1,000 feet in length, cost £5,000. For a Sussex watering-place Bognor is remarkably quiet, but it will doubtless commend itself to some people on this account'.

Tenby was described thus in a Victorian guidebook of 1895: 'Tenby stands on a tongue of limestone rock, ending in a green promontory, which is crowned by the ruins of the old castle, and is now pleasantly laid out with walks which serve at once as pier and promenade, and from which are commanded fine views of the bays on either hand … Both on the north and south sands, which are separated from each other by the Castle Hill and harbour, there are numerous bathing machines'.

ON THE BEACH 1890
Tenby, Dyfed 28062

THE SANDS 1887
Weston-super-Mare, Somerset
20318

Swings, Punch and Judy, and to the left, the Castle Coffee House Refreshment Tent, all served to attract the visitor to this seaside resort. People do not dress up in their finest clothes for the beach nowadays, but one thing that has not changed is the fact that entertainments then, as now, would have you dipping into your purse. Weston-super-Mare sits at the edge of the Bristol Channel, opposite the nature reserve island of Steepholm. Its huge tides mean that holidaymakers may have to walk a considerable distance out across the sands to even paddle.

THE SANDS 1891
Rhyl, Clwyd 29151

This is how a guide to seaside resorts of 1895 described Rhyl: 'Not many years ago there was no town here at all, but merely a few fishermen's huts upon the shore. The sands, which are extensive enough to give the full benefit of ozone to those who avail themselves of its health-giving properties, form an excellent bathing-ground, entirely free from danger. Hence Rhyl has become noted for the number of children that visit it, and these little ones find an inexhaustible fund of pleasure on its beach.'

THE PROMENADE 1899
Morecambe, Lancashire 42860

A Victorian guidebook, published in 1895, described Morecambe thus: 'Morecambe is much frequented by trippers from the busy towns of Lancashire and Yorkshire, for whose recreation are provided abundant entertainments of a distinctly popular order. There are swimming-baths and assembly-rooms, and a People's Palace … There is a large pier, a tramway, and a kind of Rosherville Garden with a lake for boating.'

THE BAY 1886
Scarborough, Yorkshire 18240

A magician entertains a crowd of well dressed Victorian holidaymakers on the beach. The town has been popular for centuries; as a spa town it was known as 'the Queen of watering places', and it has always been a healthy, bracing and fashionable resort. The town has a mixture of architecture, with the ruins of a 12th-century barbican and keep, and Regency and Victorian buildings.

THE ESPLANADE 1886
Redcar, Cleveland 18131

With Redcar Pier in the background, horses and carriages wait to take families on a sightseeing tour along the sea front. One of the bathing machines, which were introduced here in the 18th century by Charles Turner, a landowner, can be seen to the left. The lady on her three-wheeler looks quite at ease pedalling along.

THE COBB 1912
Lyme Regis, Dorset 65040

This fine study of the Granny's Teeth steps on the Cobb shows the setting of the incident in Jane Austen's novel 'Persuasion' where Louisa Musgrove falls off the wall. Jane Austen visited the town and adored the setting, capturing her enthusiasm in her novel. 'The young people were all wild to see Lyme', she wrote as her characters approached the town.

THE YORKSHIRE PIERROTS 1912
Clacton-on-Sea, Essex 64237A

Pierrot shows arrived in England in 1891. Fred Pullan's Yorkshire-based touring troupe opened in Clacton in 1901. An early handbill described them as 'Up to Date – Thoroughly Refined'. The show came to an end when a gale destroyed the stage in August 1912. By this time, in any case, Pierrots were being supplanted by non-costumed 'fol-de-rol' entertainers.

History and Heritage

STONEHENGE 1887
Wiltshire 19797

This monument is an epic feat of prehistoric technology, bearing in mind the way the stones are put together and that the stones were brought from miles away. Trying to find the origins and significance of Stonehenge has captivated historians, archaeologists and laymen for centuries.

MAYBURGH HENGE 1893
Eamont Bridge, Penrith,
Cumbria 32935

Just south of Penrith, Mayburgh Henge is a circular bank of earth and stones of about 1.5 acres, with one 10ft stone at the centre. It is thought to have been built between 1000BC–2000BC. There were four standing stones at the centre during the 19th century.

EXCAVATIONS c1908
Avebury, Wiltshire A80501

The Avebury stone circle is the largest henge monument in Britain. A later excavation of the great ditch was carried out by H St George Gray in 1922, when he established that Avebury was built in the Neolithic age. Flint tools, pottery fragments, human and animal bones and deer antlers (used as picks) were found.

THE CASTLE 1902
Saltwood, Kent 48830

Built in 1154 by Henry de Essex on the edge of a valley, this lofty castle became the residence of the Archbishops of Canterbury. Here, on a dark night in 1170, four knights met with Randolph de Broc, the then tenant, to plan the murder of Thomas à Becket, and from here they set out the next day to accomplish their mission. The keep was restored as a country mansion in 1882, and subsequently became the home of art historian Sir Kenneth Clark.

THE CASTLE 1893
Richmond, Yorkshire 32275

Richmond's Norman fortress was begun by Alan the Red of Brittany in 1071 and dominates the entrance to Swaledale. At that time, the border between those firmly under Norman control and those still willing to fight lay just a few miles to the north. Alan was the son of the Count of Penthievre, and related to the Duke of Brittany, a relationship that often saw the castle declared forfeit to the Crown. On the right of this picture is Scolland's Hall, dating from c1075 and probably the oldest domestic building in Britain. The 12th-century keep is on the north side. The curtain walls are built on a triangular pattern because of the shape of the site.

CASTLE HILL 1914
Windsor, Berkshire 66981

Queen Victoria's Golden Jubilee statue of 1887 replaced a market cross, and it emphasises the 'company town' nature of Royal Windsor – the castle has been a royal residence sine 1075. The keep (with the flagpole) was raised to three storeys and the outer walls and towers refaced in the 1820s; the walls still look remarkably fresh today.

Haddon Hall belongs to the Duke of Rutland. The hall's beginnings were in the 12th century. It was unlived in from 1740 for nearly 200 years; then sympathatic restoration began in 1912, taking some 20 years to complete. In the last century it was used as a location by film producers.

THE ENTRANCE TOWER 1886
Haddon Hall,
Derbyshire 18630

THE HERMITAGE 1896
Bridgnorth, Shropshire 38136

Bridgnorth and its castle sit on a cliff of very soft sandstone. Over the years dwellings were carved out within the stone and, as can be seen from the curtains in the windows, these were occupied into the 20th century. Though the roof sits heavily and the door tips drunkenly, they were doubtless dry and comfortable.

CHATSWORTH HOUSE AND THE FRENCH GARDENS c1870
Derbyshire 5226

Here we see the east front of Chatsworth from the French Gardens, now with pillars removed and known as the Rose Garden. The gardens were almost exclusively the work of Joseph Paxton, the Duke of Devonshire's gardener and architectural genius, who went on to design London's Crystal Palace.

By the time of this photograph, the old wharves along the river had been cleared away to create Victoria Embankment Garden, a more fitting context for the Mother of Parliaments, which was rebuilt in Gothic style between 1839 and 1860 by Pugin and Sir Charles Barry. Beyond Victoria Tower is the great royal abbey, Westminster Abbey, with its pair of west towers and the centrepiece of the medieval palace, along with Westminster Hall.

THE HOUSES OF PARLIAMENT 1908
London L130149

LONDON BRIDGE c1880
London L1303429

This bridge was designed by John Rennie, father and son. Completed in 1831, it replaced the 12th-century bridge of nursery rhyme fame; this had lasted for over six centuries – the houses built on it were finally removed in 1762. This later London Bridge pictured here was demolished in 1968 and re-erected in the USA at Lake Huvasu City in Arizona.

PLACE HOUSE INTERIOR 1888
Fowey, Cornwall 21255

This interior demonstrates the typical decorative taste of a wealthy Victorian. Heavy drapes, an ornate fireplace and ceiling, heavily patterned carpet and wallcoverings, and large chandeliers dominate the room. Beautiful ornaments, photographs and objects fill every available shelf, complimenting the slender, often tapestried chairs.

VANDERBILT'S COACH 1886
Reigate, Surrey 18968B

A party, dressed in their finery, with the ladies in large flowery hats, are on an outing on a coach owned by the millionaire Alfred Gwynne Vanderbilt. His fortunes stemmed from his family's involvement in the expansion of New York. Although his business was in banking and railways, his great love was coaching, and his coach travelled daily to and from Brighton.

Getting About

THE GREAT WESTERN RAILWAY WORKS
1913
Swindon, Wiltshire S254607

Here we see workers leaving the Great Western Railway yard, which, at one time, employed 12,000 people. The uniformity of dress amongst the men is striking. The sheer size of the building indicates the importance of Brunel's railway to the town. Gas street lighting was common at the time.

THE BOX TUNNEL 1904
Corsham, Wiltshire   51492

Isambard Kingdom Brunel built the famous Box Tunnel in 1841 as part of his ambitious Great Western Railway link between London's Paddington station and Bristol's Temple Meads. The 120 miles of railway line took five years to complete. Limestone from the excvavated tunnel was used for building houses in nearby Corsham.

THE RAILWAY STATION 1909
York, Yorkshire 61850

The magnificent sweep of York station dates from the completion of the Doncaster-Selby-York line. Opened in 1877, the station allowed through running of trains. The old station it replaced lay just within the city walls; its site and layout were such that trains had either to back in or out of it.

THE S & D RAILWAY NO 1 1892
Darlington, County Durham 30646

Designed and built by George Stephenson, Stockton and Darlington No 1, 'Locomotion', achieved a speed of 15mph when he hauled the 34-wagon inaugural train from Shildon to Stockton on 27 September 1825. This engine was later converted to petrol.

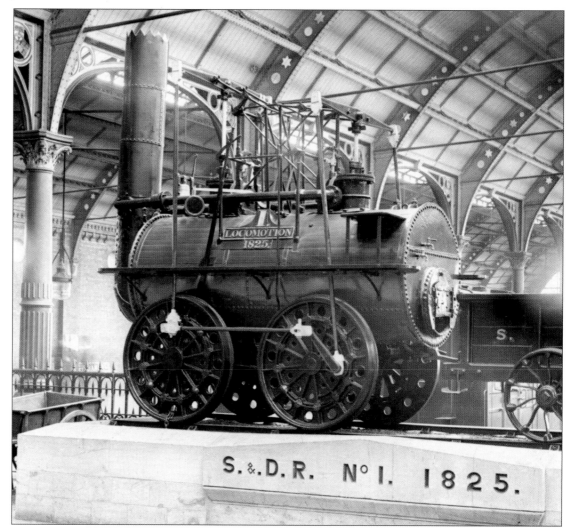

When the railway came to Grange-over-Sands in 1857 it signalled the town's rapid expansion as a seaside resort for visitors from the industrial mill towns of Lancashire. Here engine 12501 steams along the front, past the town's park, where the conical-roofed bandstand is prominent.

THE RAILWAY 1929
Grange-over-Sands,
Cumbria 82781

THE QUAY 1923
Appledore, Devon 75145

Full tide brings its own burst of activity, as small passenger boats in an orderly seamanlike manner position themselves to approach the slipway. Wicker baskets carried by the ladies (in the right-hand rowing boat) were very much a feature of life until quite recent times. This boat is awaiting its turn to come alongside, once the other two have been sculled a safe distance from the water-soaked landing place. Ladies at this time continued to be handicapped by long swishing skirts.

WALNEY BRIDGE 1912
Barrow-in-Furness, Cumbria 64407

Shipbuilders swarm across the Walney bridge from the dockyards at the end of a wortking day. It resembles scene from Lowry. A crane at Vickers dockyard can be seen in the distant background. Protected by the enclosing reef of Walney Island, Barrow flourished as a major shipbuilding centre in the 19th and early 20th centuries.

THE TRANSPORTER BRIDGE 1913
Middlesbrough, Cleveland 66412

The building of this extraordinary bridge was discussed in Victoria's reign, but it was not opened until 1901. Pedestrians and vehicles cross by means of a suspended platform which moves to and fro across the Tees. The bridge is often closed when high winds make it dangerous for use.

Sea and Maritime

THE LIGHTHOUSE 1892
New Brighton, Merseyside 30413

*O*wing to the frequent heavy seas, the Perch Light, which had stood on Perch Rock since 1683, was often washed away, and so in the 1820s Liverpool Corporation decided to build a more substantial lighthouse. It was built from granite to a height of 90ft, and is a masterpiece of engineering skill. Its revolving light was claimed to be the first of its kind in England.

THE HARBOUR 1894
Fleetwood, Lancashire 33968

*F*leetwood became England's principal fishing port on the west coast with a fleet to rival those of Hull and Grimsby. In this picture there are trawlers and Morecambe Bay prawners. The trawlers were carvel built, with an oak keel and frames and pine planking. Usually crewed by four men and a boy, they trawled for plaice, sole, haddock, and cod. The Morecambe Bay prawner, also known locally as a half-decker, shrimper, or nobby, was a cutter-rigged smack. They were fast and possessed excellent sea-keeping qualities.

THE FERRIES 1890
Devonport, Devon 22462

Plymouth and Devonport were served by a number of ferries, including these wonderful steam-powered, chain-guided floating bridges on the Torpoint service, which were capable of carrying wheeled vehicles. Services operated were Ferry Road to Torpoint (fares 1d and 2d); the Barbican to Turnchapel and Oreston; Admiral's Hard to Cremyll (Mount Edgcumbe); and Mutton Cove to Cremyll.

THE DOCKS AND CLIFTON BRIDGE 1900
Bristol 45555

A screw tug prepares to assist a steamer to its berth in the Floating Harbour. Bristol became a major centre for the importation of timber for use throughout the west of England. In 1870 it handled 105,000 tons, and by 1900 it was dealing with over 170,000 tons a year. Annual tobacco imports through the docks rose from 349 tons in 1880 to 2278 in 1910, and by the mid 1920s the average was 24,000 tons a year. As well as tugs, other service vessels included dredgers and lighters.

CHARLESTOWN HARBOUR 1912
St Austell, Cornwall 64784

The process involved in loading or unloading ships can be seen clearly here. Cargo is off-loaded from and to horse-driven wagons along wooden gullies directly from and into the hold of the vessel. The solid lock gates leading into the inner harbour allowed the water levels to be adjusted during any state of the tide, enabling either repairs to be undertaken or the dock to remain flooded at low water.

THE FISH PONTOON 1906
Grimsby, South Humberside
55750

In its day, Grimsby was the biggest fishing port in the world. Here, the local fish merchants wait alongside creels of freshly landed cod to start bidding for the best fish.

THE QUAY 1929
Wells-next-the-Sea, Norfolk
81996

From Wells to Blakeney, a great sand barrier holds back all but the most vicious tides. The quay at wells is now stranded a mile from the open sea. The Wells whelkers are renowned for their persistence. Dropping pots from open clinker-built boats in pitch darkness and foul weather meant the whelkers could often find themselves stranded for hours on end on the wrong side of the bar waiting for the tide.

THE DOCK 1893
Grimsby, South Humberside 33272

Grimsby is a major port, lying at the southern entrance of the River Humber. The Fish Dock was built in 1893, when it served the biggest fishing fleet in the world; this fact might seem to be contradicted by this preponderance of merchant vessels berthed in the Royal Dock. The mixture of power-driven ships, barques and other craft indicates the trend at the turn of the century in marine transport from sail to steam.

THE HARBOUR 1888
Polperro, Cornwall 21270

*B*uilt in a narrow gully in cliffs 400 feet high, this was once a smuggling village. Many of the fishermen's cottages looking towards the harbour were built in three storeys, the ground floor being used for storing and salting their catches of fish. The living quarters and bedrooms were reached by an exterior flight of stone steps.

Padstow is a very ancient port and has long been associated with trading and shipbuilding. In the Middle Ages silt formed the Doom Bar and cut off the harbour for the larger sailing vessels, but Padstow still continued to be a very important trading port. The vessel we see here is tied up at berth, so perhaps its sails are up to enable them to dry out.

THE HARBOUR 1888
Padstow, Cornwall 21214

NORTH LANDING 1886
Flamborough Head,
North Humberside 18001

*V*illagers wait with their baskets for the boats to come in with their catches of herring. In the middle of the 19th century there were 30 fishing boats here, but they had all gone just after the First World War. The treacherous seas here have claimed many lives, and hundreds of seafarers are buried in the graveyards.

BAITING THE LINES c1900
Staithes, Yorkshire S176001

Staithes, on the north-east coast of Yorkshire, was a fishing port of some standing. It landed sufficient cod, mackerel and haddock for the North Eastern railway to run three or four special fish trains a week. Lining was one of the methods by which the fish were caught.

FISHERMEN'S COTTAGES 1897
Newhaven, Fife 39137

These cottages at Newhaven, Fife, are an example of the type of fishermen's dwelling that could be found around harbours from Scotland to at least Cullercoats in Northumbria, usually single-storey terraces with slate or stone roofing. On the west coast of England, the old fishing communities tended to be housed in cottages with thatched roofs. At Newhaven the fishermen's wives were noted for the way they dressed, which was said to reflect the community's Dutch and Scandinavian origins.

THE HARBOUR 1885
Whitby, Yorkshire 1885 18168

This view is taken looking north across the harbour. High on the hill are the abbey ruins and over to the left, the lovely Norman church of St Mary. The church is reached by a climb of 199 steps that leaves the fittest visitor beathless. The official name for the stairs is Church Steps, but they are known locally as Jacob's Ladder. Captain Cook lived for nine years at Whitby learning sailing skills. His two ships that sailed to the South Seas, the 'Resolution' and 'Endeavour', were built here. In Victorian times many of theWhitby men were engaged in whaling, for which they had to sail far out to sea.

INDEX